The Greatest Hog Farm
I Ever Worked On

Dennis Meadows

Illustrated by: Cheryl Wald

The Greatest
Hog Farm
I Ever Worked On

Dennis Meadows

Copyright @2021 by Dennis Meadows

All rights reserved. No part of this book may be reproduced in any form or by any electronic or mechanical means, including information storage and retrieval systems, without permission in writing from the publisher, except by reviewers, who may quote brief passages in a review.

This publication contains the opinions and ideas of its author. It is intended to provide helpful and informative material on the subjects addressed in the publication. The author and publisher specifically disclaim all responsibility for any liability, loss or risk, personal or otherwise, which is incurred as a consequence, directly or indirectly, of the use and application of any of the contents of this book.

WORKBOOK PRESS LLC
187 E Warm Springs Rd,
Suite B285, Las Vegas, NV 89119, USA

Website: https://workbookpress.com/
Hotline: 1-888-818-4856
Email: admin@workbookpress.com

Ordering Information:
Quantity sales. Special discounts are available on quantity purchases by corporations, associations, and others. For details, contact the publisher at the address above.

Library of Congress Control Number:
ISBN-13: 978-1-955459-25-9 (Paperback Version)

978-1-955459-26-6 (Digital Version)

REV. DATE: 17.05.2021

INTRODUCTION

The Greatest Hog Farm I Ever Worked On This book is about like some of the others that God has helped me to write. I really want children to learn to obey their parents.

We know in Ephesians 6:1-3 it says "Children obey your parents in the Lord for this is right. Honor thy father and mother, (which is the first commandment with a promise); that it may be well with thee, and thou mayest live long on the earth."

It is a lesson God wants us to learn. Lord willing, this book will help children and adults. I believe it has a great message, even to the world. It is what God's people are to do: reach the world with the gospel. It is really a commandment because God's word tells us to. In Mark 16:15-16 Jesus said "Go ye into all the world and preach the gospel."

This book is true as best as I can remember. As I said in some of the other books, it seems I was to be a farmer. All of God's people are really farmers; many may not know it. Many do not want to get their hands dirty today with hands on work like in the church or other places.

We will start with the words of Jesus in Matthew 13:1-9. He explains about the farmer and seeds. We are planting seeds every day. One way is by the words we say, good or bad, and where we say them.

Now comes the good part. I was five years old. My dad always planted a garden. Of course, I followed him about everywhere. I was still sleeping in Dad and mom's bed and it was about that time they moved me out. One day, my dad went out to the garden. I think it was big, but at that age everything was big. With seven children, of course, a garden was needed. I saw him working in it, and said, "Dad, I will help you" so I started pulling little weeds.

We moved several times and, of course, at the age of twelve grandma Meadows gave me twenty five hens. We also got seventy five baby chicks, and they were all roosters.

We ate chicken for a long time. We would ring their necks and hang them on a fence until the blood an out. Then we would take very hot water and take the feathers off.

It wasn't long after that my dad found a large old farm house that we rented. It was a couple of miles from a tiny town called Essex, Ohio. The place had about three acres of land and an old barn with it. It wasn't long before I was helping bale hay and straw.

One older farmer had a few hogs and I would go and help clean the manure out. He was the main deacon of the church and had a very filthy mouth. He may have been saved but only God knows. It wasn't long until I helped several hog farmers.

My friend's dad had about two hundred hogs and I would go there sometimes after school. We would go and feed the hogs and cattle that they had.

Then we would go eat supper, which was usually some kind of roast with carrots, potatoes, etc. We usually had fresh lemonade with it.

Then one day, I was asked to help one of the largest hog farms in the whole area, maybe the state at the time. They had over two thousand and five hundred hogs. With that many hogs, they needed help. The man and his wife had two sons like the story in the Bible in Luke 15:11-32.

We must understand that hogs are dirty animals and the hog pen can be very dangerous. Hogs love the mud holes. When they get washed the run right back into the mud hole; sort of like lost people. The mama hogs are called sows.

My job was to feed about two hundred sows when I first arrived at work. The daddy hogs are called boars, and I was told not to get very close to them. Most of the time I stayed fifty feet away or more from them.

The sows I fed weighed two hundred and fifty pounds to six hundred pounds or more. Many people think that hogs do not get huge but some get over one thousand pounds if kept a few years.

During this time, I had bought a couple of little pigs and raised them and they had pigs. We had a cow and a calf and we milked the cow every morning and evening.

 I used some of the milk to feed the pigs since we would get about two and a half gallons every time we milked. During the summer at the hog farm we harvested the corn we planted in the spring and we put up a lot of straw.

Three years later

They had about six little buildings that they would raise little pigs in after they were weaned. In a few days the buildings would be full of manure. And we would take a pitchfork and clean them out. It would take all day long after we got our regular chores done. The job was dirty because the manure was three feet or deeper. Later on after I had left that job the smell stayed with me over thirty days.

It seemed to me that it wasn't very long before I was at my Uncle Reese's and aunt's house in Sulphur, Louisiana. After I had been there a few days, I went outside and at the back of the house in the field was an old hog pen. I guess it was about ten in the morning. I thought that would be a good place to sit and think.

Well that is what the prodigal son did; he had to think. In Luke 15:15-32 it tells us how he knew he could go back to his father's house. I sat on that old hog pen for several minutes, maybe ten or more. Then all of a sudden, I felt the Holy Spirit come down, not only upon me but all around me greatly.

I could hear a voice; it was as if Jesus was right there beside me, and it said "I am the way, the truth and the life: no man cometh unto the Father but by me", as in John 14:6. At the same time, the serpent was saying to me to say no. It seemed he was trying to show me the whole world. It was something like he showed Jesus in Luke 4:5.

The Holy Spirit told me that this would be the last chance to get saved and if I didn't that I would die and go to hell forever.

I bowed my head and asked Jesus to come into my heart, and he did and I felt a great burden lift off my soul, it was because when Jesus came in, sin could not stay in my heart. It was the most joy I have ever felt.

The greatest hog farm that I have ever worked on was not the two thousand five hundred hog farm. Oh! No! It was the world of people, and people of the world. We are all like the prodigal son, although we may not have sinned as much, but without Christ, people go to Hell. We are all lost sinners before we are saved as in Romans 3:23 "for all have sinned and come short of the glory of God".

How Long Will it Be?

By Dennis Meadows

How long will it be, before Christ my King and Savior
I shall see?
The One whose nail-scarred hands
Reached down and saved
A wicked sinner like me.

How soon shall it be?
Very soon from what the Holy Spirit tells me.
For I believe The Father is about to say to His Son,
Son, it is time!
Then the King of kings and Lord of lords shall stand
And walk out upon Heaven's portals
And say, come up hither today!

How long will it be? How long before the Lord will return?
His coming cannot be soon enough for me.
His coming will come sooner than most people expect it to be.
For the Bible says, When you see all these things coming to be,
Like we, today, plainly see
Look up for then, your savior you will see.

How will all this be? Quicker than you can see a twinkle
In your eyes that you can barely see.
How long will it be? Not very long!
How long is that? You may say.
It may be noon, night, or day.

Christ will come as a thief when most souls will not be ready.
Peace, they will say, as they are saying even today.
Eat, drink, and be merry just as in Noah's day. Then the Bible
Says, Look up, for your Redemption draweth nigh.

www.ingramcontent.com/pod-product-compliance
Lightning Source LLC
Chambersburg PA
CBHW061108070526
44579CB00011B/174